Developing Emotional Intelligence

90 Minute Guides

Michelle N. Halsey

Silver City Publications & Training, L.L.C.
P.O. Box 1914
Nampa, ID 83653
https://www.silvercitypublications.com/shop/

ISBN-10: 1-64004-017-X
ISBN-13: 978-1-64004-017-5

Contents

Chapter 1 – What is Emotional Intelligence?

Emotional Intelligence is a part of you that affects every aspect of your life. Understanding the root causes of your emotions and how to use them can help you to effectively identify who you are and how you interact with others.

With Emotional Intelligence being a fairly new branch of psychology, its definition can be found in various theories and models. We are presenting a definition influenced by a few theories, and mainly popularized by Daniel Goleman's 1995 book Emotional Intelligence.

Self-Management

In order to effectively achieve your overall career objectives or the objectives within a given task, you must use clearly defined methods to carry out those activities. This includes the setting of goals, decision making, planning, and scheduling. Once the tasks are completed, you must evaluate the success of these methods.

The following is a list of five key points to remember to help you master the art of self-management.

- Be consistent. Part of managing oneself is the ability to be stable. The values you hold dear should always be transparent. Always changing can not only cause others to question your beliefs, but it can also cause you to become confused about what you truly believe.

- Stick to the plan. If you are scheduled to complete a particular task, do it. Don't just do it, but make sure it is done in a timely manner. It is easy to feel out of control when you disregard the plan you are to follow.

- Be accountable. There are times when things don't work out as you plan, but you have to be able to admit that and then use your flexibility to get things back on track. The ideal result is that you easily bounce back and complete the task, but even during those times when this is not the case, you are expected to adjust.

- Educate yourself. We live in an ever-changing world and you want to be able to keep up with it. Don't let change pass you by, embrace it. Be an avid reader. Talk and listen to mentors and peers. They may know something that could help you along your journey.

- Stay physically fit. Many people don't think of staying fit when they talk about self-management, but it is a very important part of being able to practice the four preceding points. Exercising your body is just as crucial to self-management as exercising your mind. A body that is not well rested, nutritionally fed, or physically exercised can lead to emotional and physical illnesses.

Self-Awareness

Being 'aware' of one's self is the ability to accurately perceive one's skills and knowledge, value and responsibilities. It is being confident in what you have to offer, whether it is personally or professionally.

Self-awareness is not only important for one's self-esteem, but it is also the first step to the process of full acceptance or change. Without understanding why one thinks the way he thinks or why he acts the way he acts, he may never fully appreciate himself or see the importance of making changes to improve him, if necessary. Self-awareness gives power and a sense of peace or happiness. This newly found strength will more than likely carry over into your work life, how you perform your duties as well as how you interact with others.

The lack of self-awareness can cause you to not realize your worth in the company or even the quality of the work you perform. This can have an even more dramatic effect when you hold a leadership position. Not only will you have doubts about yourself, but the people you lead will also begin to question your competence, which could ultimately lead to a lack of leadership effectiveness.

Self-Regulation

Self-Regulation is another term for 'self-control', which is defined as the ability to control one's emotions, desires, and behaviors in order to reach a positive outcome. Self-regulation is sometimes difficult because of the phenomenon that it is important to 'express how you feel'. While this may be partially true, the art to finding the balance between expressing one's feelings and avoiding unnecessary tension is self-regulation.

Self-Regulation is a direct reflection of the type of pressure one is experiencing. There are three types of pressure:

- Good Pressure: This type of pressure is the result of an aggressive yet non-critical and non-harmful atmosphere. One aspires to be like the people around them. This motivation leads to the acquisition of self-regulation.

- Bad Pressure: Bad pressure is the when the atmosphere is critical and harmful. One has no motivation and loses self-regulation.

- No Pressure: When one is not experiencing any pressure, they tend to act based on emotion, since there is no one to compare themselves to.

Self-Motivation

Andrew Carnegie said it best with his quote "People who are unable to motivate themselves must be content with mediocrity, no matter how impressive their other talents." Self-motivation is an essential part of excelling at life. You must learn to motivate yourself because you cannot depend on others to do it for you. You have to know how to encourage yourself regardless of how bad the situation. There are several keys to building self-motivation.

- Work towards a cause.

- Don't compare yourself to others.

- Make the conscious effort to not give up.

- Don't live in your past failures or successes.

- Utilize positive thinking.

There are times when you may need motivation to get motivated. Positive thinking may not be doing the trick. What should you do? Consider these suggestions:

- Write down your plan for improvement.

- Briefly think about your past successes.

- Read books that promote self-motivation.

Empathy

Empathy is sharing in the feelings of others, whether joy or sadness is an admirable trait. In order for empathy to work, a person must first be able to recognize, classify, and understand their own feelings.

Empathy has been defined by others as:

- Alvin Goldman: The ability to put oneself into the mental shoes of another person to understand her emotions and feelings.

- Martin Hoffman: An effective response more appropriate to another's situation than one's own

- Carl Rogers: To perceive the internal frame of reference of another with accuracy and with the emotional components and meanings which pertain thereto as if one were the person, but without ever losing the "as if" condition. Thus, it means to sense the hurt or the pleasure of another as he senses it and to perceive the causes thereof as he perceives them, but without ever losing the recognition that it is as if I were hurt or pleased and so forth.

Empathy is most useful when the one empathizing has experienced a variety of feelings. For example, the boss who was once passed over for a promotion generally finds it easier to identify with another person who is passed over for a promotion. Not only is this comforting for the person who is going through the situation, but it's also good for empathizer because it strengthens their ability to positively react to negative situations.

It is not as simple as it sounds. The ideal situation would be for a person to express their issues and you empathize with them, but the fact is, people aren't always as forthcoming with their problems, even though it is obvious that there is something wrong. Since this is the case, you may be forced to ask probing questions or read between the lines of what is said. You can also focus on non-verbal cues such as body language.

Chapter 2 – Skills in Emotional Intelligence

Developing successful Emotional Intelligence begins by understanding your emotions and their meanings. With this understanding, you must uncover productive ways to manage your emotions, then use them to the benefit yourself and others.

How to Accurately Perceive Emotions

The words that people say are only half of the message they are trying to get across. The tone in which they say it, or the emotion tied to their words, is the other half. For example, if your boss says, "We're going to have to let you go" with the look of concern or in a caring tone of voice, he /she are actually saying, "Unfortunately, we are going to have to let you go." On the other hand, if your boss makes that statement, trying hard to keep from laughing, he / she could be saying, "Fortunately, we are going to have to let you go."

The ability to decide the manner, in which things are being said, lies in your knack of being able to decode the message by looking beyond the words themselves. It is important that you do not allow your emotional state of being to cloud your judgment of what is being said. Focus on the message (verbally and non-verbally) itself in order to accurately perceive the emotions of others.

Use Emotions to Facilitate Thinking

'Use emotions to facilitate thinking' is such a profound statement. How one feels will determine how he/she views situations. If you are in a happy mood, everyday events don't seem so bad. On the contrary, if you are not in a happy mood, even the smallest of situations can seem major to you.

When it comes to the workplace, regardless of your mood, your boss expects you to be a high performer. Make it easy on yourself and 'choose' to be in a good mood.

Understand Emotional Meanings

The underlying reason for why you feel the way you do is very important to understand. If you know why you are unhappy, you can either alter the thing that is making you unhappy or consciously tell yourself that 'thing' is not worth allowing you to be upset, which can ultimately turn your negative mood into a positive one. Having this understanding can not only be used to internally gauge yourself, but can also help with how you interact with co-workers.

Chapter 3 – How to Accurately Perceive Emotions

Knowing what emotion you are exhibiting or understanding the reason for that emotion is not enough to manage your emotions. Managing your emotions is a conscious and active task. This can be done in several ways. The overall goal is to establish strategies that utilize your emotions to help accomplish a goal rather than allowing your emotions to use you to create a futile outcome.

It is important to remember that your emotions are not the 'enemy'. They contain valuable information that if used properly, can help you make sound decisions.

Verbal Communication Skills

Strong verbal communication skills are important in all facets of life. Without these essentials, one may find it hard to get a personal point across, articulate needs and desires or even compete in the business world. There are many factors that contribute to solid communication skills.

Focused Listening

One of the best ways to ensure someone that you are truly listening to what they are saying is to intently listen. To some this may sound like common sense, but it is a skill that is seldom mastered. Usually when engaged in a conversation, the listener is multitasking. They are listening with one part of the brain and preparing a response with the other. It is painfully obvious when a person is not wholeheartedly interested in what someone else has to say. Not only does this make the listener look uncaring, but it may also influence the speaker to go elsewhere when he needs to speak about matters.

Whether you are in a leadership role or an individual contributor, strong listening skills are essential to your success. Hearing something other than what is being said or trying to think of what to say while the speaker is talking, can have dire consequences. Regardless of the industry you work in, focused listening is a great skill to sharpen.

Asking Questions

Asking probing questions is a component that goes hand-in-hand with focused listening. Rarely does someone truly understand everything another is saying without at least asking a couple of probing questions. The key is to not ask questions for the sake of asking questions, or ask questions that do not relate to the conversation. For example, Amy talks to Michelle about a project they are going to work on together. The goal of the project is to create a high school lesson plan for a literature teacher. Michelle has never created a lesson plan and has no idea of what is included in one. The conversation is as follows:

Amy: Hi Michelle. Today we are going to prepare a lesson plan for a high school literature teacher. This lesson is for the book, Teaching to Transgress: Education as the Practice of Freedom. It is not necessary for you to read the book. We have a summary and analysis for each chapter, which is sufficient to develop the plan. There are several sections of the lesson plan that we have to write and it has a non-negotiable deadline.

Michelle: Great, Amy. I look forward to writing the lesson plan with you; however, I have several questions:

- Specifically, what are the sections that we must create?

- Is there a template or certain grammatical rules that we must follow?

- In what format do we complete the lesson plan?

- What is the final due date?

Amy felt like she adequately described the assignment and how it should be done, but because Michelle was listening carefully, she had the opportunity to ask several probing questions to gain a better understanding of what was to be done.

Communicating with Flexibility and Authenticity

When speaking to another, the one rule you want to always observe is that you are being honest about what you are saying. This can be somewhat of a challenge because we are taught to speak with diplomacy; being politically correct, especially in the business-world. While this is true, it is still necessary to make sure you are not sugar-coating or dancing around an issue, as this can cloud the meaning of what is being communicated. Effective communication does not require the speaker to repeat or continuously restate what is being said.

Even though sometimes one is as honest or clear as they could possibly be, it takes a little more work to relay the message. The ability to be flexible in your speech, whether to make your meaning more clear or to 'show off' that diplomacy you have been working so hard at, is significant for verbal communication success.

Non-Verbal Communication Skills

There is more to communication than the words one speaks or message being conveyed. There are also non-verbal cues that all use in everyday conversations. Being mindful of the signals you send others through body language and the manner in which you speak may get your point across a lot faster than your mere words.

Body Language

The saying, 'Actions speak louder than words' is so true in the world of business. It is easy to shower someone with promises, but when it is time to perform, if the actions do not measure up to the words spoken, the words spoken will be forgotten.

The use of body language can have both positive and negative effects. The thing to remember about body language is that if you are not conscious of what your body is doing while you are talking, the wrong message could be conveyed. For example, if you are smiling while giving someone condolences on the loss of their loved one, that could be construed as inappropriate and your words insincere. On the other hand, if you are congratulating someone on a job well done, but do so with a frown on your face, you could appear to be unhappy for the person.

The signals you send to others.

Sending non-verbal signals to someone can be a great way to reinforce that which you've verbally spoken. It can also be used as a tool to further explain what you're trying to say. However, it can be a way of confusing the listener. So, this can be a valuable skill as long as you are conscious of it and have trained it to have a positive effect rather than using it as an uncertain form of communication.

Chapter 4 – It's Not What You Say, It's How You Say It

The manner in which you say something could be the factor that determines what the listener hears. It is important to be aware of your emotions, body language, tone, speed, and pitch when you speak. It may sound like a lot of work and until it becomes second nature, it may be, but consistently doing so can produce a favorable outcome. It is possible to send the wrong message without intentionally doing it, so be careful. An innocent request such as 'Please shred that document' can sound like a rude command.

Social Management and Responsibility

The terms Social management and responsibility refer to a group or organization's participation in environmental, ethical, and social issues outside of the organization itself. 'Outside of the organization' can refer to issues at the country level, B2B (Business to Business) level or even the individual development of the members within the group or organization.

Benefits of Emotional Intelligence

Emotional intelligence is *"the ability to perceive emotions, to access and generate emotions so as to assist thought, to understand emotions and emotional knowledge, and to reflectively regulate emotions so as to promote emotional and intellectual growth* (Mayer-Salovey, Four Branch Model of Emotional Intelligence).

Focusing on the importance of Emotional Intelligence and developing EI skills serves many benefits. Specifically, it affects one decision-making ability, relationships, and health.

- **Decision-making.** Having an awareness of your emotions, where they come from and what they mean, can allow you to take a more rational, well-planned approach to how you are going to make a specific decision.

- **Relationships.** When one is able to understand why they are the way they are and why they react to things the way they do, they tend to gain more of an appreciation for others and who they are, which can in turn lead to stronger relationships, business and personal.

- **Health.** Many times, internal turmoil expresses itself as physical illnesses. Always harboring negative emotions can lead to higher stress levels in the body, which can temporarily or fatally damage it.

Articulate your Emotions Using Language

As a child, it may be acceptable to 'act out your emotions' to get your point across, but when you become an adult it is frowned upon and certainly not appropriate in the work place. Emotions will never go away, but that is not an excuse to say, do and behave anyway we want to. It is important to understand your emotions, what they are, and why you feel that way, and then share your feelings via positive and constructive conversation.

When in a leadership role, you may encounter several opportunities to express yourself, whether it is praising a worker for a job well done, or reprimanding an employee for not meeting deadline. But the key to making sure you articulate your emotions in an effective and efficient manner is to channel those emotions so that your message comes across as firm but professional.

Chapter 5 – Tools to Regulate Your Emotions

The ability to keep your emotions under control requires more than a willing heart. Understanding a situation through the eyes of another and strengthening self-management and self-awareness skills are tools that can be used in your quest to regulate your emotions.

Seeing the Other Side

If you ever want to understand the type of person you are and how you behave, ask other people. It is easy to justify the things you do, so much so that it seems like everything you do is perfect. If you take an honest look at yourself, you would probably say not only is this perfection untrue for you, but it is unattainable for all.

Talk to your boss, co-workers or friends about how they view you. If someone says, 'When everything is good you are a nice person, but if something doesn't go your way, you have an explosive temper', don't get upset and don't automatically say that it is untrue. Gaining this insight is a valuable tool for you to help regulate your emotions. Your emotions and how you express them is your responsibility. If you don't like it, fix it.

Self-Management and Self-Awareness

Self-management can sometimes be a hard quality to tame when self-awareness produces a very arrogant and self-centered result. The strength to self-management and self-awareness lies in the balance between the two. Understanding who you are, the role you play, authority you possess are all very important, but when these things overshadow your ability to be consistent and accountable, this could cause a poor outcome. By the same token, if one lacks understanding of whom they are and their importance, this could also hinder their ability to be consistent and accountable. People who are aware of their methods of dealing with conflict and understand the bearing of their way of doing things aren't as likely to make matters worse than those who are not aware of themselves.

Giving in Without Giving Up

Compromise is an unavoidable part of dealing with others in both the business world and in personal relationships. The ideal situation would be that everyone agrees with everything you say, but that is highly unlikely. Unless you live in a society that does not value diplomacy, this is a skill that will present plenty of opportunities for you to master it.

This can be even more of an issue when you are in a position of less influence. You may be expected to compromise at a greater level or even expected to follow the lead of your superiors, without regard to your own feelings or opinions. In either case, learning how to have your beliefs, while accepting the ideas of others and not causing tension in the relationship is crucial to your success in the work place.

Gaining Control

Just by the very nature of the word, control is a very powerful thing to have. Having control causes companies to become multi-billion dollar entities and nations to crumble. This is no less important when it comes to having control over yourself, your thoughts, and emotions. Having control or the lack thereof could be the difference between building a successful career and no career at all. If you have control over these aspects of your life, pat yourself on the back. If you do not, read the following to obtain the necessary tools to become the master of your fate.

Using Coping Thoughts

The power of the mind is amazing. Every day, you will encounter at least one situation that requires you to use the calming forces of your mind, to overcome the potential anxiety of the issue at hand. In order to use these forces, you must have a reservoir that consists of them. When you find yourself in a situation that requires coping skills, do the following:

- **Take a deep breath.** Deep breathing has an amazingly calming effect on the brain. By taking a deep breath or two, you can easily avoid your first, natural reaction to a stressful situation. This can prevent you from saying something or physically acting out in a manner that is inappropriate and may require you to apologize later on.

- **Step away from the issue.** Mentally take yourself away from the situation and analyze the issue itself. Ask yourself if it is something worth using your emotions on. Does it truly impact you? Will your emotions bring forth a resolution to the problem or just internal conflict for you?

- **Use positive thinking.** Even if the situation requires you to physically act, you do not want to approach it with thoughts of anger, sadness or other negative emotions. Consciously tell your mind to think 'happy thoughts'. Thinking happy thoughts is not a way to avoid the problem, but rather a way to prepare you to tackle it in a productive manner.

Using Relaxation Techniques

Relaxation techniques are not just used to help you 'feel better'; they actually play a major role in reducing the stress on your body and mind that comes from the experiences of everyday life.

According to the Mayo Clinic, relaxation techniques can reduce stress symptoms by:

- Slowing your heart rate

- Lowering blood pressure

- Slowing your breathing rate

- Increasing blood flow to major muscles

- Reducing muscle tension and chronic pain

- Improving concentration

- Reducing anger and frustration

- Boosting confidence to handle problems

There are several common types of relaxation techniques, with three of them being:

- **Autogenic:** This technique uses the senses to promote relaxation. For example one may think about a peaceful place and then use relaxed breathing. Or they might repeat words in their mind to do away with muscle tension.

- **Progressive muscle**: In this technique, individuals purposely tense and then relax each muscle group.

- **Visualization:** With visualization, the individual imagines a calming place and tries to utilize his or her senses to feel like they are really at that place.

Bringing it All Together

Once you have mastered the art of coping with difficult situations, it may not be necessary to engage in relaxation techniques as much. But until you have reached that point and maybe even afterwards, finding effective ways to relax yourself and take control of the situation is highly beneficial. Whether it is dealing with an unruly co-worker or a demanding boss, not allowing negativity to get the best of your emotions can benefit your mind, body and soul, which is the ultimate goal.

Chapter 6 – Business Practices

There is more to the workplace than the business itself. An employee's makeup, which is emotions and their ability to manage them, level of Emotional Intelligence and communication skills are all a part of whether or not a business is successful.

Understand Emotions and How to Manage Them in the Workplace

As previously stated, having emotions is an inherent part of all human beings. Understanding one's emotions and learning how to use them is the responsibility of each person. Many times, it may feel like the workplace is no place for emotions, whether good or bad. But the truth is, emotions must be utilized!

For example, if you are the manager and your team is about to miss an important deadline, it is up to you to stress how necessary it is for you to meet the deadline. The approach you take is determined by your natural tendencies as well as level of professionalism. One level-headed approach may be to call the team to a meeting and explain the ramifications of not meeting the deadline. This would also be a good time to listen to the team members to find out if there is something out of their control that is preventing them from doing their job.

A less calm and volatile method would be to yell at everyone and tell them to get to work.

Deciding which style is best can be done by weighing the pros and cons of each as well as which would result in the most positive outcome. Do not rely solely on how you feel, but what makes logical sense.

Role of Emotional Intelligence at Work

Emotional Intelligence plays a vital role in the workplace. How one feels about himself, interacts with others, and handles conflict is directly reflected in the quality of work produced. Both social and personal proficiencies are developed as a result of Emotional Intelligence.

Social Proficiencies

- Empathy – Being aware of others' feelings and exhibiting compassion.

- Intuition – An inner sense of the feelings of others'.

- Political Acumen – Ability to communicate, strong influence and leadership skills, and conflict-resolution.

Personal Proficiencies

- Self-Awareness – Understanding one's own emotions. The ability to asses one's self as well as display confidence.

- Self-Regulation – Managing one's emotions. Maintaining trustworthiness and flexibility.

- Motivation - Being optimistic about situations. Having the drive to take initiative and commit until completion.

Disagreeing Constructively

To disagree constructively means to do so in a positive, productive manner. Its purpose is not to disagree for the sake of disagreeing or getting your point across. It is also not used to be negative or destructive of another's thoughts. The workplace is a place where disagreeing is a common occurrence. Companies look for the most effective ways to carry out operations and therefore invest in process improvement strategies, which opens the floor for discussion and compromise.

What does constructively disagreeing look like in practice, you may ask. Well, it is acknowledging and confirming someone else's ideas before presenting your own.

Example:

Ted: Because of the nature of their duties, I feel the customer service phone team should arrive 30 minutes before their shift to bring up their systems and test their equipment to make sure it is properly working so they are ready to take the first call as soon as their shift starts.

Michael: I understand your point, Ted and I agree the phone team should arrive early to prepare themselves for the start of their shift. However, I feel 15 minutes is sufficient time for them to get everything in place.

Optimism and pessimism are two schools of thought adopted by individuals within organizations. Neither extreme is considered better than the other. The proper balance of the two is a fundamental part of best business practices.

Optimism

Possessing the quality of 'optimism' is the ability to find the bright side of every situation. This is an admirable position that not all have. The secret to exhibiting this characteristic is to understand that there are no issues that cannot have a positive spin.

Not only is this beneficial for an individual's personal life, but optimism can be a competitive advantage in the business world. Like every other entity, businesses suffer losses and setbacks, but the trick to maintaining the stability of a company is leadership that knows how to look past the current problem to a nearby resolution. Optimistic employees tend to be more productive in terms of the quality and quantity of their work and therefore make more money for the company.

Who wants to follow a leader that whimpers at the sight of trouble just like the people he is leading? Not many people can honestly say they desire this type of leader.

Optimism is also good for your health. There have been several studies performed that conclude those who live life with a bright outlook, generally live longer than those who do not. Also, optimists are likely to have more long-lasting, successful personal relationships.

Pessimism

Pessimism is the exact opposite of optimism. Instead of viewing the glass as 'half full' or having a positive outlook on situations, pessimists can only see the down side of the issue.

As you would expect, pessimism in the workplace can be very detrimental to the individual's career growth and the well-being of the company as a whole. A pessimist who holds a leadership role can bring down the productivity and morale of the team, just by his or her very nature. An individual contributor with this type of attitude may never get promoted to leadership positions.

What about the health factors associated with this pessimism? Pessimists generally suffer a lot of bodily and mental stress, which can manifest itself in a variety of ways such as heart disease, diabetes, and even cancer. So what's the moral of the story? Don't worry, be happy.

The Balance Between Optimism and Pessimism

Extremism may not be a desirable trait in a person. This is also true when it comes to optimism and pessimism. Being optimistic about every situation could potentially lead a person away from reality and taking the proper steps to resolve a situation. It could also give someone a false hope, which would ultimately lead to disappointment which could in turn cause the person to abandon all optimism.

Chapter 7 – Making an Impact

There are opportunities we face each day that allow us to make an impact on the lives of others. How we impact others is up to us. It requires a conscious effort on our part to decide if we are going to leave a legacy of good or bad. Whichever you decide, be sure to thoroughly think through who you are and what you want others to remember about you.

Creating a Powerful First Impression

Although some don't like to admit it, many are greatly concerned with the first impression that is made to a new acquaintance. The impact one leaves can be the difference between getting and not getting a job or obtaining and not obtaining a contract for your company. There are several factors to keep in mind when meeting someone for the first time, whether it is through electronic means or face-to-face.

Physical Appearance: It is unfortunate but true that when you are in a face-to-face meeting, you are initially judged on your physical appearance. Always err on the side of caution and present yourself in a conservative light. Avoid flamboyant clothing, jewelry, and make-up. Even though you may be confident in your abilities, these things can send the message that you are unprofessional and not capable of performing the job.

Body Language: Many times, body language speaks so much louder than words. From posture to facial expressions, the message being conveyed can be completely different from the intended message. So, it's important to be aware of how your body is positioned as well as the messages it gives. In addition to posture and facial expressions, be mindful of your eye contact and the tone, pitch and speed of your voice.

Although posture and eye contact may not be as important when you are communicating on the phone, your facial expressions can be very apparent. Smiling while talking is an easy thing to do that says you are professional.

The first handshake should be firm enough to show you are confident, but not so firm that it cuts circulation to the other person's fingers. Be sure to include good eye contact while you are shaking hands.

Spoken Words: This is one of the more obvious but neglected aspects of the first impression. Focusing too much time on your physical appearance or body language can cause you to forget to choose your words carefully. Choosing your words carefully is not about you withholding your true self, but remembering there are some situations that require you to be more politically correct or proper. Stay away from the slang you would use with friends or in other less formal situations. Also avoid using too much jargon or words not typically used in everyday language, as this may cause the listener to tune out what you are saying for the mere fact that they cannot understand you.

Assessing a Situation

Before deciding on the path to take to approach a situation, one must first assess it. Is it worth doing anything about? How will it impact me or others? The overall goal is to be effective when dealing with issues, so make sure you know what you are getting into before embarking on the journey.

The best way to assess a situation is to step away from it. Take yourself out of the equation in order to fully understand what it is about and the effect it will have. This can allow you to make a more reasonable decision rather than one based on emotions.

Being Zealous without Being Offensive

Being a zealous person is a good quality, but being overly zealous can not only send a negative message to others, it may be considered offensive. Every manager would like to hear that their employees are excited about work. This sends the idea that the employees will focus on 'getting the job done'. However, 'getting the job done' is not the most important thing, 'getting the job done' correctly is. The drive to work fast can be a down fall of being overly zealous, as sometimes the individual may lose the focus on quality. The positive side is this individual can bring to the team a renewed excitement that was once lost.

With everything in life, you must strive for balance, not extremism on either end of the spectrum. This balance will not only bring internal stability for you, but it will also allow you to maintain equilibrium within your relationships.

Additional Titles

The 90 Minute Guide series of books covers a variety of general business skills and are intended to be completed in 90 minutes or less. It is an effective way for building your skill set and can be used to acquire professional development units needed by project managers and other industries to maintain their certification. For the availability of titles please see

https://www.silvercitypublications.com/shop/.

No. 1 - Appreciative Inquiry

No. 2 - Assertiveness and Self Control

No. 3 - Attention Management

No. 4 - Body Language Basics

No. 5 - Business Acumen

No. 6 - Business and Etiquette

No. 7 - Change Management

No. 8 - Coaching and Mentoring

No. 9 - Communications Strategies

No. 10 - Conflict Resolution

No. 11 - Creative Problem Solving

No. 12 - Delivering Constructive Criticism

No. 13 - Developing Creativity

No. 14 - Developing Emotional Intelligence

No. 15 - Developing Interpersonal Skills

No. 16 - Developing Social Intelligence

No. 17 - Employee Motivation

No. 18 - Facilitation Skills

No. 19 - Goal Setting and Getting Things Done

No. 20 - Knowledge Management Fundamentals

No. 21 - Leadership and Influence

No. 22 - Lean Process and Six Sigma Basics

No. 23 - Managing Anger

No. 24 - Meeting Management

No. 25 - Negotiation Skills

No. 26 - Networking Inside a Company

No. 27 - Networking Outside a Company

No. 28 - Office Politics for Managers

No. 29 - Organizational Skills

No. 30 - Performance Management

No. 31 - Presentation Skills

No. 32 - Public Speaking

No. 33 - Servant Leadership

No. 34 - Team Building for Management

No. 35 - Team Work and Team Building

No. 36 - Time Management

No. 37 - Top 10 Soft Skills You Need

No. 38 - Virtual Team Building and Management

www.ingramcontent.com/pod-product-compliance
Lightning Source LLC
Chambersburg PA
CBHW071344290326
41933CB00040B/2330